Destined Desires

Published By

Destined Desires

Written by Dr.Niveditha Preeth MDS

Published by : Poetry World Org.

Publisher's Address : Haryana

Printed under PWO in India

 Special credits to Dr.Nitin Chopra.

Edition : I (2021)

ISBN (Paperback) - 978-93-92507-10-6

Book Design by POETRY WORLD

Destined Desires

Written By

Dr. Niveditha Preeth MDS

PROLOGUE

A tale of two souls,

Bound together by friendship.

Like the opposite magnetic poles,

They glued with each other.

Was it a friend?

Or was it a foe?

Who had put an end,

To their innumerable struggles.

Was it Friendship,

That had won?

Or was it Love,

That was shunned?

Far from the South,
He set out his sail,
For his fated future,
Where he would prevail.

Life took a new turn,
Away from his sweet home,
With his new crazy friends,
In the tiny hostel dorm.

Missing family and friends,
He had bitter days at the start,
In his new professional college,
He felt a void in his heart.

Little did he know,
Love would find its way,
Cooling his heart like snow,
With just a small 'hey'.

Delicate as a rose,
Naive as a child,
She followed the path,
Her family had chose.

Out of her protective shell,
She stepped in the new world,
To learn her lessons for life,
And those life's altering spells.

With a new hope,
Towards a fresh start,
In a place so new,
Filled with excitement, she hopped.

A tiny game, destiny had planned,
To play with her fragile heart.
Little did she know,
The cruel twists fate had planned.

On a bright sunny day,
The campus bustled with students,
All smiling wide in gay,
To start a journey afresh.

In a well furnished air-conditioned hall,
Sat the students one by one,
Waiting for their names to be called,
To give their intros to all.

On a chair far behind,
She sat looking around,
The strange faces of humankind,
From distant lands and towns.

A row in the back of her,
He sat with his new found mates.
In came a few nerdy professors,
Smiling warmly at their new batch.

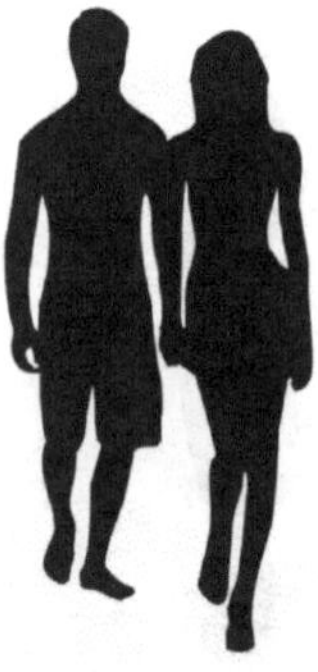

A little here,
And a little there,
Her eyes wandered,
Away from the boring speeches.

A little behind her, he sat,
Lost in his own thoughts.
In the long crawling class,
He glanced at her spot.

A slight turn she had taken,
And their eyes had found their ways.
The sleepy hearts had waken,
With a sweet hello.

The warm smile and the sweet hello,
Was all it took for him,
For his fondness to flow,
Towards his new found mate.

Sometimes a warm smile and nod,
Sometimes a silent and sweet hai,
Had been their way to greet,
Not forgetting to end with a bye.

'He seems to be nice',
Was what she thought,
'She is so good',
Was what he thought.

I wish I could talk,
But, how do I start?
What will I talk?
Had been their confusing part.

Knowing they would always hesitate,
Destiny decided to help.
On a boring lecture day,
They had taken their first step.

On vital practical hours,
Into batches they were split,
For the cadavers to be slit,
And the lessons to be learnt.

With her at the last,
Both were put apart,
Disappointment hit their heart,
As their wish was to be with each other.

Luck had cast its charm,
With the entry of new member,
They were put together,
And their grins expressed their joy.

As days rolled on,
Lectures gave a hard time,
Yet, their hearts synced in rhyme,
As they sat side by side.

Busy professors took their stroll,
Each step resonating loud,
In the silent dissection lab,
Amidst the sleepy crowd.

Secrets slips were passed by,
Silly pranks were laughed at,
All behind the teacher's back,
By a few naughty lads.

Looking at his smiling face,
A small smile adorned her lips,
Laughing at his petty jokes,
She enjoyed the class with those tricks.

An inch closer they had moved,
A little more than 'hai' and 'bye',
Feeling at ease, they spoke,
Building a new bond thereby.

Her eyes would always roam,
In search of him in the room.
Wandering lonely as a cloud,
Her sight would land at his crowd.

All laughing merry and gay,
She would often find him at bay,
Her heart would always dream,
For him to call her a team.

Eager glances they would share,
Often a smile, here and there.
In fright of what others would say,
Unspoken they would end the day.

A little more than hai and bye,
A little into the life of her guy,
She slipped, deciding to end the wait,
Words were exchanged near and straight.

One fine day, bored of the silence,
She took her phone, texting some,
Far from behind, he saw her chat,
And curious he became as a cat.

Finding a perfect time,
He sneaked past the line,
Mustering some courage,
He asked her enraged.

When and how did you buy?
Why wouldn't you notify,
The handy mobile's digits?
He asked wasting no minute.

Keeping her books aside,
She smiled and replied,
A few days ago,
But had no one to show.

Those were the times,
Of Nokia and Samsung's chimes,
Androids were nowhere,
And chatting was very rare.

A lot of pleading,
And a lot of saving,
It took her to convince,
Her mom to buy this tiny prince.

Fewer were her friends,
Lesser were her texts sent,
Deeper in her heart,
She wished for him to start.

And that destined day,
She saw his text say,
A beautiful morning's wish,
Replying, she blushed at his wish.

In his isolated land,
Surrounded by his clan,
He sat wondering who
Would initiate the words few.

Waiting, waiting and waiting,
He was tired of the betting,
Taking out his tiny phone,
He played in the safer zone.

Receiving a reply,
He released a relieving sigh,
And the threads went on,
For a while, long and long.

Mom's call was her cue,
For her night curfew,
Ending the talks abrupt,
Their hearts, smile did corrupt.

From then on, they moved forth,
Messages exchanged back and forth,
Not quite often, but at times in need,
Of a friend who would heed.

She, was always hesitant,
To initiate the first step,
He, would always take the lead,
Though he never liked the deed.

Her interest he wished to know,
His interests she wished to grow,
Both unaware of the bonding hearts,
Pretended to stick on to the friends part.

Days passed and the texts turned to calls,
Secretly she would pick them all.
Sharing her secrets, hidden to the rest,
He slowly became her safer nest.

Amidst the uncaring crowd,

Who were just a passing cloud

She befriended him close

And he bonded to her the most.

Life was filled with joy,

With his clan, for the boy,

While for the lady doll,

It was like obstacles standing tall.

Days filled with party, fun and friends,

His sophomore year came to an end,

Nights filled with restless dreams,

Her years passed like the flowing stream.

On a fateful day,

Destiny decided to play,

And their days together,

Seemed to wither.

As the lot feared,
Their exams neared,
Into the books they were cocooned,
Hoping to get the words tuned.

Days passed and results hit hard
Few on the move and few barred
Lot messed up the ranks
Yet they continued the little pranks.

She was on the move,
While he got held up with his crew,
Few chances of meeting
Now had become rare and fleeting.

Programmed robots, they had become,
Passing each and every class numb,
With her batch she formed a bond,
To pass the years not so lone.

Every now and then,

Her thoughts would drift

To the days spent with him

Secretly gazing at him.

He, often exchanging texts,

Would feel wholesome with her.

Continuous chats or calls

Was what he would prefer.

Though on the other,

She had her trouble,

With her fam, interrupting often,

Yet, she'd manage the chats and calls.

Without him in her class,

Her yearning for him intensified,

For even the slightest sight,

Would give her immense delight.

Days passed fast,
And then came a day,
A day of celebration,
For the college fest.

Her heart bubbled in delight,
For he would be there in the light,
Amidst the crowd with his gang,
To witness the fun filled fest.

Eyes scanning the crowd,
Lips curved up in joy,
As she spotted him,
Cheering for his mates.

Discrete she moved closer,
Standing by his side, talking slower,
While the huge crowd roared aloud,
Their hearts too drummed loud.

As the year neared its end,
Her fear to score too did end,
She did become bold and brave,
And a lot did change in the final year.

Their heartstrings ripened,
And the bond had fastened,
A bit more than friends,
Yet, not closer to love.

She did crave for him
And he for her,
Sadly both never expressed
Their feelings so intense.

On his special day, she gifted his favorite.
The chaos she went through to purchase,
Flew away, as she saw his content smile,
A trouble worth going through.

Crazy she may be,
To gift something
She had yearned for him
To be far away from.

Something she wished he hadn't done,
Something she wished he hadn't sipped,
Was what she had given him,
To express her love, though not direct.

She was precious to him,
A friend he dared not to lose,
Opening up to her,
Was as easy as a pie.

Moments shared with her,
Was what he treasured to the core,
Though he loved his girl,
Words were left unsaid in fear.

As if tired of the wait,
And the unsaid words' weight,
An opportunity fate did create,
For them to communicate.

A trip to the hills,
Filled with chills and thrills,
The batch had set a date,
For it was their last moments of fun together.

Hours of pleading, gave its fruits,
For her fam had finally let her free,
In joy to spend the trip with him,
She hopped and hoped to cherish.

Alas! There she was disappointed,
At the unfortunate twist.
He had planned to skip,
This final little trip.

Not losing hope, she tried to persuade,
Yet, he was firm in his stand.
All came crashing down,
When she knew it was just her.

She wished to create memories,
With him in the final moments,
Without him, she felt barren,
Though surrounded by her friends.

All was set, for the trip to start,
Luggages packed and decked,
Transit bus geared and ignited
At the marked night, moon shining bright.

One by one, the guys took their seats,
And her eyes still searched for him,
Sadly hoping for him to enter,
Luckily, dampened mood turned bright.

Her eyes glimmered in joy,
As she saw him entering at last,
That's how destiny decided to play,
With their desires by the end of the day.

The crowd cheered loud,
And the music blared aloud,
Echoing through the nights
Was the party fueled in joy.

Her eyes kept drifting to him,
But his gang kept him occupied,
She hoped for his text
Or at least a little nod.

But, nay! He was all silent and hard,
Talking and sleeping with his gang.
Half way through, a small smile they shared,
As their eyes met, piercing the crowd

Moments later, at the break of dawn,
For a coffee they had stopped.
Taking it as a cue,
She slowly drifted from her friends.

Hoping to find him alone,
She scanned the rejuvenating gang,
A little away from his friends,
He came apart for a talk.

Happy with the small chat,
She enjoyed with her batch,
Moving bodies with the blaring music,
Laughing loud like a crazy maniac.

Tired of the fun, the batch decided to rest,
All silent in their own nest.
Sleepless, she sat awake,
Thoughts of him clouding her.

Moments later, at the break of the dawn,
For a coffee they had stopped,
Taking it as a cue,
She slowly drifted from her friends.

Hoping to find him alone,
She scanned the rejuvenating gang,
A little away from his friends,
He came apart for a talk.

Happy with the small chat,
She enjoyed with her batch,
Moving bodies with the blaring music,
Laughing loud like a crazy maniac.

Tired of the fun, the batch decided to rest,
All silent in their own nest,
Sleepless, she sat awake,
Thoughts of him clouding her.

Resting the night,
They planned for the day.
Out around the hills,
They wandered creating memories.

Here and there, along the way,
Few talks and smiles,
Made their hearts,
Crave for more.

Snaps as she wished,
Talks as she yearned,
Exploring together as she craved,
Cupid had granted them all.

With his gang, she did roam,
Around the hills and the steeps,
His friend teasing all the way,
She did bond with them, though not strong.

And then came the night,
Of the planned campfire.
Not tolerating the cold,
His jerkin, she did borrow.

Safe and warm, she felt,
Inhaling his scent.
Together around the flaming fire,
They nestled against each other.

They crooned to the tunes
And danced liked goons
Round and round
Around the incensed inferno.

Under the canopy of twinkling stars
And the moon shining bright
It was a night to remember
In the month of cool November.

The night was special
Love lingering in the air,
Closeness surging high,
With a lot getting tipsy and high.

Many had retired to their beds,
While a few were out in the dark,
Relishing the cold night
With their closed ones.

She with him and he with her,
Shared their moments of fun,
His friend sensing the love,
Dismissed her to retire to bed.

Half-heartedly she did depart,
Leaving the guys to their glee,
Reminiscing the moments with him,
She slept scrolling through the snaps.

The last day around the hills,
She sat with him throughout,
Cherishing every moment,
With satisfied smiles.

The day was long,
And hearts so heavy,
For every mate's wish,
Was for the trip not to end.

Reluctant, the batch did return,
Driving down the hills,
Music still blaring loud,
And bodies swaying in tune.

Smooth and soft, fate hadn't wished,
Hence, on that dreadful night,
On the way back home,
An unfathomable incident befell.

The night was dark and hazy,
Thick blanket of mist rolling,
Thrills running down the spine,
She felt as if venturing into the unknown.

Though hearts drummed in fear,
Excitement too pumped clear,
A journey worth remembering,
It was, in her monotonous life.

Roads blocked, vehicles jammed,
Long queue of lights flickered,
Awaiting their turn,
To get back on the wheels.

Tired of the wait and the jam,
The boys got down to help,
Directing the vehicles in dark,
And that's when fate played its cruel card.

Cheering crowd grew silent,
Voices outside echoed,
Directing the traffic,
He got down too, to help.

Moments passed, wheels moved slow,
On the small safety parapet wall,
He stood with his guys,
Helping the wheels clear.

An unnerving feel, she sensed,
As if something grim was bound to transpire,
In fear, her eyes were fixed on him,
Praying for the guys safety, especially him.

Within a blink of an eye,
From the slippery wall he slipped,
Falling into the pit,
Hanging on to the roots for life.

His core had an erratic race,
For a moment he thought,
It was his end,
And so, did she.

All they had was only prayers,
Hoping the guys would pull him back.
Shutting her eyes tight,
She stood inside the bus, helpless.

The guys on the other,
Tried hard pulling him up,
Alas! It was not easy as thought,
Tears clouded the couple's eyes.

Never losing hope, the guys tried their best,
Grabbing long clothes from the girls,
They did pull him up,
Finally, breathing a sigh of relief.

Jams were cleared,
And the transit was set on wheels,
Towards the destination,
Where everything started.

All silent and calm, after the storm,
He sat amidst the crew,
Who were calming him down,
Afar, she stood, eyes fixed on him.

Tears threatened to cascade,
Gulping down the treacherous drops,
She sat, watching the passing trees,
Alone, heart drumming in fear and relief.

Many thoughts of losing him,
Clouded her making her grim,
That's when she realized,
Her profound love for him.

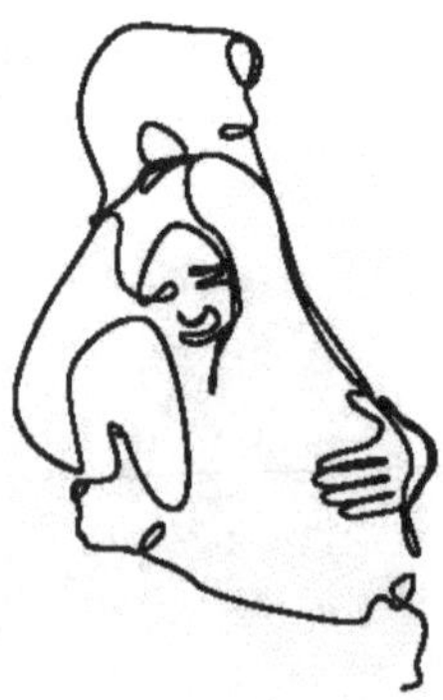

A while later, he sat,
Near her in the empty seat,
Starting a little chat,
Hoping to calm the edgy nerves.

Calm smile hiding the storm in the eyes,
Adorned the couple's lips,
Fingers interlacing with each other,
Found solace in the enjoined warmth.

Arms encircled tight,
A little closer they sat,
Shoulders in a close embrace,
They savored the passing moments.

A short break later,
The mates resumed their rejoice,
Pulling the two souls too,
Who sat snuggling lost in their world.

It was the end of her college life,
The last day of goodbye.
They met exchanging glances,
Smile concealing the inner turmoil.

At the day break,
They traveled their own paths,
Far off from each other,
Hoping to never lose the other.

His sane friend who had their love sensed,
Cut the chase and spat the words straight,
Though he had his crush,
He dared not to lose her trust.

He wished not to rupture the bond
They shared, mistaking it for love.
Nothing more to say, his friend nodded,
Coming in terms with the reality.

In her path, she wandered,
Venturing her passion.
In his path, he strolled,
Tying the loose ends.

Unexpected he had to stay behind,
With his fellow mates few,
Loitering in the grounds of college,
Signing off terms to end.

Occasional meets they had planned,
A simple talk in the café
Or a ride afar in his bike,
Creating memories to linger in the mind.

He was the one, she would stay in touch,
And he on the other was no less,
Both crazy for each other,
Were fools blinded by fate.

The clock ticked tocked,
In him her heart was locked,
But, she wasn't prepared,
To break the bond for love.

She kept thinking about him,
After everything that had happened,
Especially after the trip,
She decided to take the risk.

Though she feared,
Her gut did insist,
He too had strings attached,
With her heartstrings.

That silent night, alone in her room,
She dialed his number,
Heart racing fast,
Breaths rapid and high.

Half expecting, the call be unanswered,
Seconds of ringing seemed long,
Her core thumped with the ringing tunes,
The lumps hard to swallow.

Her breath hitched as the call was answered,
Formal was her beginning,
A bit reluctant and then,
Hesitant she started to speak.

Unsure of what was bound to happen,
She confessed, little hope shimmering in.
Silence, as a calm before a storm,
Prevailed, answers left hanging mid.

The breaking bomb he dropped,
Confessing the truth of his accepted love,
And that's when her brain whirl pooled,
The many moments she saw him with her.

Often she wondered, who she was to him,
Another girl close to him, apart from her,
Jealousy and possessiveness would creep in,
At times she witnessed them together.

And now everything came crashing in,
Every puzzle's piece seemed to fit in,
Tears cascaded down her cheeks endlessly,
Pain tearing her apart.

Both uttered the unsaid words,
Yet, was in vain.
Both expressed their profound love,
At time, none had any gain.

For the concealed feel, blaming each other,
Both in unison said the reason similar,
To save the bond of friendship,
They had severed the bond of love.

She found it hard to let him go,
Though it was hard, he let her go.
Letting it go was the worst,
As rivers of tears had burst.

It'd crushed them to the core,
Making their hearts roar.
They desired for more,
But destiny wouldn't favour.

Elixir of his life, she was,
The blood of her heart, he was.
Together they made a great pair,
But life had always been unfair.

In their eyes, the world could perceive,
Their love that was concealed.
The days neared its end,
Marking a scar that'd never blend.

With sad smiles they did depart,
As they were fated to be apart.
Many days had passed,
Yet their hearts never surpassed.

She yearned for his texts and calls,
He on the other had built up his wall,
Tired of trying and trying,
She spent her days and nights crying.

Caught in a puddle of trouble,
He cut of his threads and crumbled,
Losing himself to the ardent spirits,
He surpassed the set limits.

A huge struggle he did go through,
To come out with flying colours,
Love on one and family on the other,
Pressured to attain their wishes.

A step higher in her career,
She had taken out of all odds.
Panicked of tying the knots,
She had made a great escapede.

After a dark phase of life,
With the help of her friend,
She emerged out,
Trying to bury the past.

New friends, new place,
And a new journey,
Yet, his thoughts often grazed,
From the deep buried memories.

Rumbling through the thorny path,
A few roses on the way, she found
The two facets of the coin,
She witnessed, learning many things anew.

Out of the blue, there was his text,
Like the good old days,
Happily greeting her,
Unaware of the torments she went through.

Pain and happiness, all came stumbling back,
Conflicts within her inner-self,
To reply or not to,
Conquered her ongoing days.

Wishing not to upset him,
She replied, though not much.
Wondering what was wrong with her,
He was upset of her new self.

Again it was he himself,
Who would initiate the talk.
Love bloomed another time,
With her, he wished to be.

A new love, was gifted to her,
Not wishing another heartbreak,
She had treasured her gift,
Right from the very start.

Scared she was again,
Of losing his friendship,
But life's lessons of the past,
Made her confess in time.

Though complicated the gift was,
The couple tried to work on the bond.
Talks of tying the knots,
Had finally begun for the couple.

He, unaware of her new strings,
Wished to mend the broken part,
Anger, jealousy and possessiveness,
A mixture of emotions, he underwent.

Though he felt the growing distance,
He knew not the reason.
She on the constant debate,
Was not wishing to break him again.

Concealing her new love to him,
Made her guilt intensify every time he spoke,
A little hint she did feel,
Of his growing love towards her.

To wander off without a word,
Would make him leave, she had thought,
But her heart didn't wish,
To do unjust to him.

Calls and texts were exchanged often,
She trying to be friends again,
He trying to convey his love,
Yet again, destiny had twisted their fate.

One fine day, she received his call,
And a text that sounded urgent,
Texting back, she called him late,
When he broke the surprise.

The surprise, which she had yearned,
In the good old days.
After years, he had returned,
To the place where he had met her.

A meet after several years, he asked,
Though she wished to meet,
She was grounded inside her home,
With no chance to step out in the world.

Determined he was to meet her,
To know her answer.
Thinking of a way to work it out,
He found a way.

To her house, with a mutual friend,
He visited her after a long gap,
Excited and happy, she was,
Nervous and silent, he was.

Jovial was her mom, mingling with him,
Lots of casual talks, teasing and fun
Her fam, treated him as theirs,
Sought was his advice too, for her career.

A while later, he bid goodbye,
She heaved a sigh, of the unfortunate day,
She wished had come long back,
Before she found her treasure.

She smiled happily, yet the guilt gnawed,
Not wishing to give him a false hope,
She decided to break the ice,
The very evening before his return.

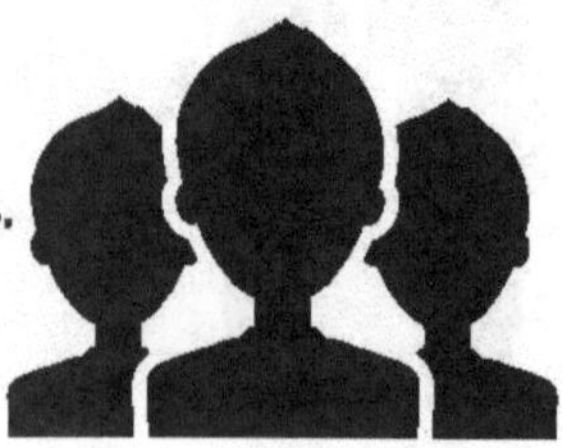

Before she could utter,
He raised his question,
Learning about her love,
From their mutual friend.

She hummed in response,
Breaking his heart,
Silence was the answer,
As his hopes shattered.

He had traveled, miles from the South,
To ask her hand as his beloved,
Alas! Destiny had played its game,
Yet again, but in his life.

Moments later, expressing their hearts,
Both realized their paths,
Smiling yet again with pain,
They returned to the point of being
friends again.

EPILOGUE

It was neither a friend
Nor a foe.
It was they themselves
Who had put an end.

Friendship or love
Neither could decide
Which had won
The journey of life.

Call it destiny or
Call it cupid's play
A strange bond they do share
With all the love and care.

Years may pass
But they'd still remain
Each other's first love
With complex strings attached.

No time is the right,
Confess when you feel the love,
You might not know,
When it's too late.

About the author

Dr. Niveditha Preeth MDS., from Salem, Tamilnadu, is a dentist by profession and a writer by passion. She has always been creative and arty by nature. Her hobbies include reading and writing stories, poems, practising arts and crafts. She believes in spreading smiles through her profession as well as her passion. She has been a contributing author of many national and international anthologies. She is also a volunteer in a non-profit international literary organisation approved by the Govt. of India. Hope and faith in her God is the one she never loses. Wandering through the horizons she hopes someday she'd find a soulful story to ink.

Follow her writings on insta @niveditha_preeth

Author's Note

Thinking of writing a book is simple but completing is harder than I thought. But when done it is far more joyous than I could have ever imagined. It took years for me to complete this book and the pleasure I felt after seeing the outcome is indescribable. None of this would have been possible without the Almighty's blessing. I'm eternally grateful to my family and my best friend Dr.Nitin Chopra who was my constant support and motivator. A very special thanks to my mentor, a father figure and well wisher Dr.Rohit D'Souza and my publishers Poetry World Org. A special mention to my friend Dr.Pravin Dhas who played a major role in helping me script this tale and also a special thanks to Akila Prabagar, Chinmay who motivated me to ink this poetic tale in the very beginning. Finally, a heartfelt gratitude to all readers who makes writers happy.